Jeff Janssen's

PEAK PERFORMANCE PLAYBOOK

50 Drills, Activities & Ideas to Inspire Your Team,
Build Mental Toughness & Improve Team Chemistry

Jeff Janssen, M.S.

Peak Performance Coach

Published by Winning The Mental Game
6841 Piershill Lane
Cary, NC 27519

Phone: 1-888-721-TEAM   Fax: (919) 303-4338
E-mail: jeff@jeffjanssen.com   Website: www.jeffjanssen.com

Acknowledgements

Selected ideas in the playbook were contributed by or adapted from: Gary Barnett, David Cook, Wayne Halliwell, Tom Hanson, Dorothy Harris, Lu Harris, Holly Hesse, Jerry Jerome, Laura Kenow, Janet Montgomery, Patrick Murphy, Lute Olson, Jack Parker, Ken Ravizza, Jim Rosborough, Pam Stone, John White, Wes Worrell.

Adapted material taken from the following sources:

Harris, D., & Harris, B. (1984). *The athlete's guide to sport psychology: Mental skills for physical people.* New York, NY: Leisure Press.

Ravizza K., & Hanson, T. (1995). *Heads up baseball.* Indianapolis, IN: Masters Press.

Warren, W. (1997). *Coaching and control.* Paramus, NJ: Prentice Hall.

Additional Resources by Jeff Janssen:

Championship Team Building (book)
The Team Captain's Leadership Manual (book)
The Seven Secrets of Successful Coaches (book with Greg Dale)
The Mental Makings of Champions (workbook)
Perform to Your Potential (booklet)
Winning The Mental Game (video)
The Psychology of Sensational Hitting (video with Leah O'Brien)
The Softball Coach's Guide to Mental Training (audio with Ken Ravizza)
Mental Training for Softball (workbook with Mike Candrea)

TABLE OF CONTENTS

50 Drills, Activities & Ideas to Inspire Your Team, Build Mental Toughness & Improve Team Chemistry
© Jeff Janssen • www.jeffjanssen.com • 1-888-721-TEAM

INTRODUCTION

Drills and Exercises for Improving Mental Toughness and Team Chemistry

Coaches and athletes intuitively know that mental toughness and team chemistry are two of the most important areas in achieving sport success. Most coaches and athletes from all sports and levels routinely rate factors like confidence, commitment, concentration, having a common goal, communication, and teamwork as contributing as much as 80-95% to a team's success. However, the majority of coaches traditionally devote as little as 5-10% of their practice time per week developing the mental game and team chemistry.

Fortunately, just as physical skills can be developed through systematic drills and exercises, so too can you develop and strengthen mental toughness and team chemistry. That's really why this Peak Performance Playbook was created - to give you as a coach 50 practical, fun, and effective drills, activities, and ideas to help you improve your team's mental game and enhance team chemistry. Many coaches enjoyed the activities in my book *Championship Team Building* so in essence, this book provides you with several more ideas.

These drills are designed to be easy, economical, and most important, effective - three things I know every coach needs in today's fast-paced, do more with less, competitive sporting world. Many of these drills can be quickly completed in only five to fifteen minutes time. Thus they can be easily incorporated almost anytime before, during, and/or after practices.

"I hear, and I forget. I see, and I remember. I do, and I understand."
Chinese Proverb

Learning by Doing

As the preceding proverb suggests, the best learning occurs when people are active. While some learning occurs through instruction and modeling, the most effective learning happens when people are actively engaged. As you know, athletes, by their very nature, are physical people who love challenges, games, and activities. Thus, this Playbook is designed to help athletes learn the way they learn best - by doing.

While your athletes will love the exercises, more importantly, they will gain critical insights and strategies that will help them be more mentally tough and better team players. Every one of these drills has been used and tested in the sporting world. They are some of the most fun, memorable, and meaningful experiences athletes have had with teams. I have included many of my favorite drills and activities as well as some that have been shared with me from coaches and colleagues across the nation. All efforts have been made to credit the sources of the activities whenever possible.

How To Use This Playbook

As you page through the Playbook, you'll notice the drills are organized by topic, much like physical drill books are organized into offensive and defensive sections. Unfortunately, because each team and situation is different, I can't exactly tell you which drills will be best for your team. It is up to you and your coaching staff to assess your team to determine the areas you need to focus on and improve. An effective way to assess your team's mental game and team chemistry is to use the Mental Game Evaluation and the Team Building Evaluation. You and your players can find both of these evaluations at *www.jeffjanssen.com* as part of my website. After completing these evaluations and seeing where you stand, you can then select one or more of the drills you think will work for your team.

Getting The Most Out Of The Exercises

Each of the drills comes complete with a drill objective, setup equipment, step by step directions to help you successfully lead the activities, and most importantly, some ideas and questions for discussion afterwards.

While the exercises will be fun and challenging for your players, the most important part actually occurs after the exercises in how you relate them to the team. Following each exercise, be sure to ask your players how they can relate what happened in the exercise back to the team. Allow each person to share an idea or insight from the exercise. Use the discussion questions to stimulate their thinking and to get the ball rolling. It is important as a coach that you let your players do most of the talking while you serve to facilitate the discussion. Also, be open to their insights and be sure they focus on solutions. Monitor any criticism that is shared to ensure that it is presented constructively.

If you are unsure of leading or facilitating the exercises or want to make sure that you get the most out of them, you might want to consider having an outside, experienced person lead the activities. (Feel free to contact me for information on my team building workshops and retreats.) Basically, you want your players to effectively use the activities as a tool to gain new and reinforced insights and strategies on what it takes to be mentally tough and to have great team chemistry.

How to Contribute Drills, Activities & Ideas to Future Volumes

Finally, my goal is to provide you and your fellow coaches with more drills and activities in the future. Thus, if you would like to contribute a drill, exercise, or idea you have found especially effective with your team to future volumes of the Playbook, please e-mail me at *jeff@jeffjanssen.com*. I will credit you as the source and provide you with a complimentary copy of the Playbook should I include your idea in future volumes.

I hope you and your team enjoy the drills as they help you build mental toughness and team chemistry!

TEAM BUILDING ACTIVITIES AND IDEAS

1. MAGIC SHOES

Objective

To help your team work together to conquer a challenge. The challenge encourages your team to problem solve, communicate clearly, determine a plan, make adjustments, decide on roles, and overcome adversity.

Setup

You will need a oversized pair of athletic shoes (two sizes larger than the person with the biggest feet) and an open area roughly 10 yards long which symbolizes the river.

Directions

The goal of the exercise is to use the shoes to transport the team from one side of the river to the other. The shoes are magical and only the person wearing them can safely walk across the river. However, each player is only allowed a one-way trip wearing the shoes. The shoes cannot be tossed across the river in any way and must travel together as a pair at all times.

Given these parameters, your players will typically assign the stronger players to wear the shoes to cross the river. They do this with a teammate on their backs and/or standing in front of them on top of the magic shoes.

Safety Precautions

As with any type of physical activity, there is always a chance of injury when doing this exercise. It is wise to walk along with your players to spot them as they cross. Also, place foam mats on each side of the walkers to help cushion a fall should it occur. Finally, be sure that any players who have weak knees, ankles, etc. do not carry people across the river.

Discussion

Who were the leaders of this exercise?
Was it better to be stronger to carry people or smaller so you could be carried?
What kind of planning and strategizing was involved?
How well did teammates support, respect, and trust each other?
How did your team deal with obstacles and adversity?

Source:

Jerry Jerome
University of Illinois

2. TEAM JUGGLE DRILL

Objective

To help your players learn how to work together. It is also a good drill when players feel overwhelmed by demands or they are having difficulty facing stress.

Setup

You will need a large open area and 6-10 balls from several sports (basketball, baseball, softball, football, volleyball, soccer ball, etc.) or any other throwable objects. Arrange your team in a large circle so that the players are roughly an arm's length away from each other.

Directions

Hand a player one of the balls and ask the player to throw it to a teammate somewhat across from them in the circle. The player should remember who they threw the ball to because they will throw it to the same person during the rest of the drill. The player who received the ball should then throw it to another teammate, again remembering who they threw to. This process continues until all the players have received the ball from one teammate and have thrown it to another. The final person to catch the ball will then throw it to the person who originated the drill.

After each person understands who they received the ball from and who they throw to, initiate the exercise again, this time adding a second ball after the third teammate has received the ball. Add another ball once the second ball gets to the third teammate and see how the group does with three balls in play. Initiate the drill a third time and this time add all the balls into the mix, adding them one at a time once the previous ball gets to the third player. Time your team to see how long it takes them to get all the balls through the team and back to the start. Also, keep track of the number of mis-throws, dropped catches, or mid-air ball collisions. Challenge your team to improve their times and accuracy by seeing how quickly and efficiently they can complete the drill.

Discussion

What were the keys to being successful in the exercise?
What did you focus on to be effective?
What messages about trust did this exercise demonstrate?
How did you respond if there were any mistakes? How did this affect your success?
Did you become more effective over time? If so, why or why not?
What did this exercise remind you about responsibility and accountability?
How can this exercise help you when you are feeling overwhelmed by too much to do?

3. BACK TO BACK COMMUNICATION

Objective

To emphasize the importance of clear communication and attentive listening. The exercise also stresses the importance of two way communication and being specific when giving directions.

Setup

Make copies of the Back to Back Communication diagrams (enough for half of your players) and provide blank sheets of paper for drawing. Arrange your players into pairs sitting back to back - one will be a drawer (have pens) and one will be a describer.

Directions

Hand the describer a sheet showing the various shapes. The drawer is not allowed to see the sheet (or the sheets used by other pairs). Ask the describers to describe the drawing in detail to their partner. The drawers should attempt to draw what is described on a blank sheet of paper. However, the drawers are not allowed to speak during the exercise. After roughly five minutes, giving the drawers enough time to finish the exercise, have the pairs compare their drawings. Typically, some drawings might be close and others will be way off base. Take a little time to discuss the exercise with your players using the discussion questions below.

Then have the partners switch roles. Hand out the next sheet of shapes to the new describers and have them repeat the exercise. This time allow the drawers to clarify and ask questions of the describer, again without actually seeing the drawing. After roughly five minutes, allow the pairs to compare their drawings.

Discussion

One Way Communication - Have the drawers discuss what it was like not to be able to clarify the instructions they were given. Also, ask the drawers what it was like not to be able to see or hear how their partners were doing. What communication principles were emphasized with this exercise? As a describer, how could you have been a more effective communicator? As a drawer, how tuned in where you as a listener? What does this exercise remind you about seeing things from another person's perspective? How did the describer's attitude and tone of voice affect the accuracy of the drawing and the feelings of competence by the drawer?

Two Way Communication - Ask the drawers what it was like to be able to clarify the describers instructions. Also, have the describers discuss the ability to get feedback from their partners. Ask your players what this exercise teaches them about communication within a team.

8

BACK TO BACK COMMUNICATION

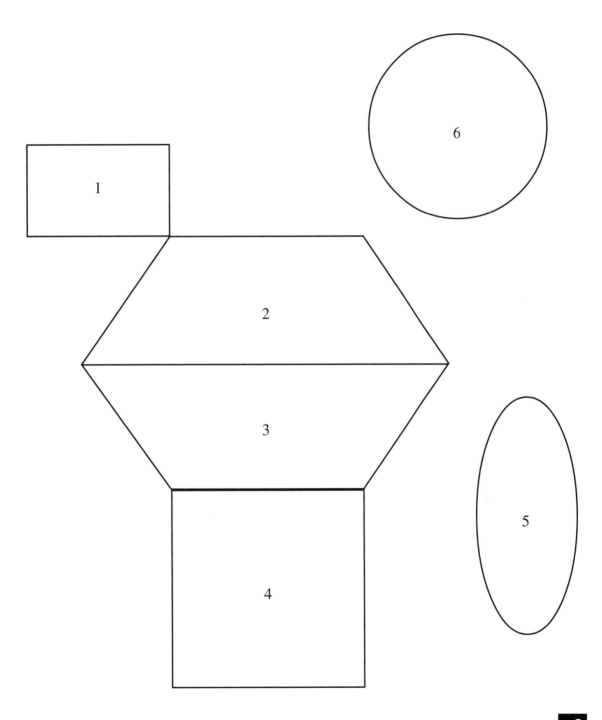

BACK TO BACK COMMUNICATION

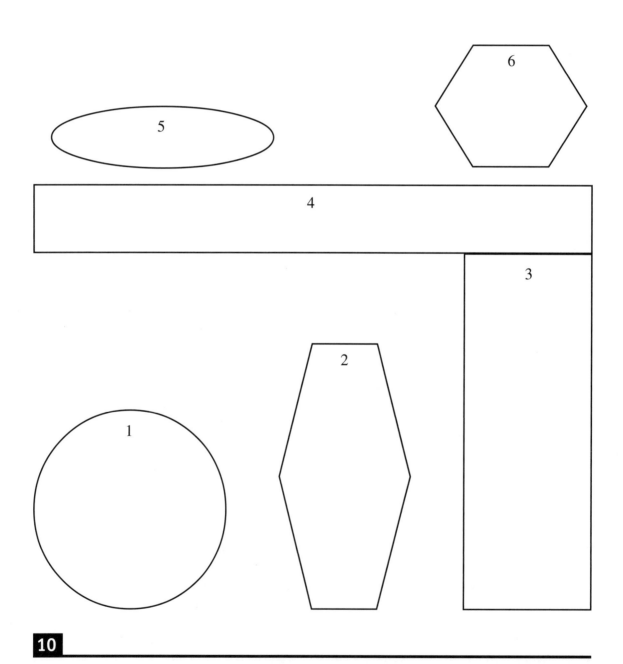

50 Drills, Activities & Ideas to Inspire Your Team, Build Mental Toughness & Improve Team Chemistry
© Jeff Janssen • www.jeffjanssen.com • 1-888-721-TEAM

4. ROCK SOLID

Objective
Rock Solid is a team building idea which emphasizes the power of unity and commitment.

Setup
Ask each of your players to collect a medium-sized river rock. You will also need some paint the color of your school colors and a large bucket.

Directions
At the beginning of practice, have your players paint all of their rocks the same school color by dipping them in paint and letting them dry. Paint the bucket as well. Then, either after practice or the following day, ask your players to paint on their rocks any meaningful quotes, individual goals, or names of people who are inspiring them this season. Each player will have their own custom-painted river rock. With the bucket, have your players paint on their team goals for the season and any inspirational slogans they might have.

Again, after allowing time for the paint to adequately dry, gather your players together in a group with their rocks in hand. Tell your players that you would like them to seriously consider their goals for the season. If they are truly committed to these goals, ask each player to place their rock in the bucket, one by one, to symbolize their long-term commitment to the team.

Discussion
After everyone has placed their rock in the bucket, show your players how tough of a task it is to move the bucket when all of the rocks are in there together. However, when taken alone, the individual rocks can be easily thrown and kicked about. Remind them that this is similar to a team. There is tremendous strength in unity, however, when players play as individuals they can be easily kicked around.

Contributed by:

Jack Parker & Wes Worrell
Bishop Kelly High School Football
Boise, ID

5. BLINDFOLDED BIRTHDAY LINEUP

Objective
To have your players creatively communicate with each other without talking.

Setup
Large open area and blindfolds for your players.

Directions
Blindfold each of your players. Then take them by the hand and scatter them around the open area so that they are at least five to ten feet away from each other. Your team's challenge is to arrange themselves in chronological order of their birthdays with January 1 being on one end and December 31 on the other. The catch is that your players may not make any verbal sounds during the exercise. Allow your players at least 20 to 30 minutes to complete the exercise. As a coach, be sure that your players do not run into any walls or anything else that could injure them.

Discussion
Ask your players what it felt like when they were separated from their teammates.
Did they think it was possible for the team to complete the exercise?
What methods did they use to communicate with each other?
How did they deal with the frustration they might have felt?

6. AUTOGRAPHS

Objective
To help break the ice when players do not know much about each other.

Setup
Devise a list of 20-30 characteristics like the one listed below. Make enough copies for each of the players and provide them with pens/pencils.

Directions
Give your players 5-10 minutes to find other team members who fit the characteristics listed. When they locate the person, they should have the person sign their sheet of paper. The players should go around and find one to three people who fit each description. You can award a simple prize at the end for the player who has the most total signatures on their sheet as well as the person who was able to get a signature for each characteristic.

Discussion
The exercise is used to help people find out what they have in common as well as getting to know each other's names. It is a great one to use in the early stages of team building at the beginning of a season.

Sample Characteristics
Find as many people you can who fit the characteristics listed below. When you locate a person, have them autograph your sheet.

Get the autographs of people who:

1. Have a dog (list dog's name)
2. Have a cat (list cat's name)
3. Wear contact lessons
4. Have won a championship
5. Have a birthday in August (list date)
6. Have a large immediate family (six or more people)
7. Had a GPA of 3.0 or higher
8. Have a relative who played a sport in college
9. Have traveled outside the U.S. (list country)
10. Favorite food is Mexican
11. Have their own website (list URL)
12. Like country music (list favorite singer)
13. Have been to Disney World
14. Have a nickname (list nickname)
15. Favorite color is blue

7. FAMILY VISITS

Objective

To help you get to know your players better by investing the time to talk with the people who typically know them the best - their parents (or guardians). This suggestion also is great for opening up lines of communication with parents and demonstrating how much you respect them and value their input and support.

Directions

Of course this idea depends on your budget and where most of your parents live. If you have a major college or professional budget or if your player's parents live near by, make an appointment to visit with each one of your player's parents in their homes. Coach Barnett suggests that you can work your travel in conjunction with your regular recruiting trips and visits. If money is tight or they live far away, you can make an appointment to speak with the parents by phone.

Discussion

Begin by letting the parents know that you appreciate their support. Tell the parents that you want to learn more about their child because you want what is best for them as their coach - both in their sport and in the game of life. Ask them to tell you about their child and let the discussion flow from there. You might want to talk about their child's goals, how they handle adversity, how they respond to criticism, what motivates them, how they get along in group settings, etc. Focus on really listening to what the parents have learned about their child. These insights will prove highly valuable to help you know how best to interact with your players.

Contributed by:

Gary Barnett
Head Football Coach
University of Colorado

8. SAFETY PIN CHAINS

Objective
To show your players that each of them is an important and valued part of the team and its success.

Setup
Purchase some large safety pins, enough for each member of the team.

Directions
Hook the pins together so that they form a large chain. Show your players the chain and talk about the strength and unity the circle symbolizes. Remind your players that they are only as strong as the weakest link. If someone breaks away from the group, the chain is broken and the unity is shattered.

Then, as a reminder of this metaphor, take the chain apart and give each player one of the safety pins to attach to a shoelace, uniform, keychain, etc. Remind them that each time they dress for practices and games, to remember that they are part of a greater team.

Contributed by:

Pam Stone
Head Softball Coach
Arizona Western College

Janet Montgomery
Head Softball Coach
University of West Alabama

9. TEAM TOUCH - STAYING IN TOUCH

Objective

To promote a sense of unity among your players and discourage cliques.

Directions

Talk about the special bond that players have with their teammates. Emphasize that this is a group of people who are willing to work hard for each other, make sacrifices, and pursue the same goals. To honor and respect the other person, encourage your players to touch each other with a high five, hug, or some special handshake or physical sign. They must do this every time they ever see a teammate (for the first time) whether they are in school, at the mall, or wherever.

Discussion

This exercise encourages players to continually make an effort to acknowledge and reach out to teammates. It is good at inoculating your team against the formation of cliques. It also is good for teammates who might be in a conflict with each other because it forces them to realize that despite the problems, they are still teammates.

The idea might take a little time to catch on. Take the lead yourself and high five your players when you see them to show that you as a coach are serious about it. Also, be willing to hold those accountable for not following through.

Adapted from:

William Warren
Head Coach
Author of Coaching and Control

10. KINDNESS CHAIN

Objective
To demonstrate how simple acts of kindness can have a positive, uplifting, and unifying effect on your team.

Setup
You will need a journal or notebook.

Directions
As the coach, begin by doing a small act of kindness for your team such as bringing them some fruit to snack on before practice. Have one of your players take the kindness baton from there and do something nice for a teammate the next day, like taking her out to lunch. The person who was taken out to lunch then continues the kindness chain and might send a teammate some flowers, write her a nice card, or carry her gear. The kind acts should continue until everyone on the team has participated.

The idea is especially effective when players do nice things for their teammates who are having a challenging week (breakup with a boyfriend, homesick, or struggling in school) or for players they don't interact with all the time.

Discussion
The person who does the act of kindness should record it in a team journal and write down how it made them feel. Once the kind acts have travelled to each member of the team, go back and read the journal as a reminder of the special things done and how it made the players feel to reach out to their teammates. Remember to include your support staff as well with your groundskeeper, secretary, equipment manager, media relations, and of course your peak performance consultant! Then start a whole new chain.

Contributed by:
Holly Hesse
Head Softball Coach
Southwest Missouri State University

DRILLS TO BUILD MENTAL TOUGHNESS

11. FREAK OR PEAK PERFORMANCE

Objective

To help your players better understand their mindset when they are performing poorly and when they are playing well.

Setup

Copy the Freak or Peak Performance sheet for all of your players and have colored markers available.

Directions

Tell your players to write and draw words, phrases, or pictures which depict their thinking when they are performing poorly (freak). Then have them do the same for when they are playing their best. Have your players share and explain their sheets with the team.

Discussion

What similarities are there between teammates when playing poorly?

What similarities are there between teammates when playing well?

Contrast the quantity of thoughts between the freak and peak side?

How much control do you have over the things listed on the freak side?

Who decides which thoughts dominate your thinking?

What can teammates and coaches do to help players think peak performance thoughts?

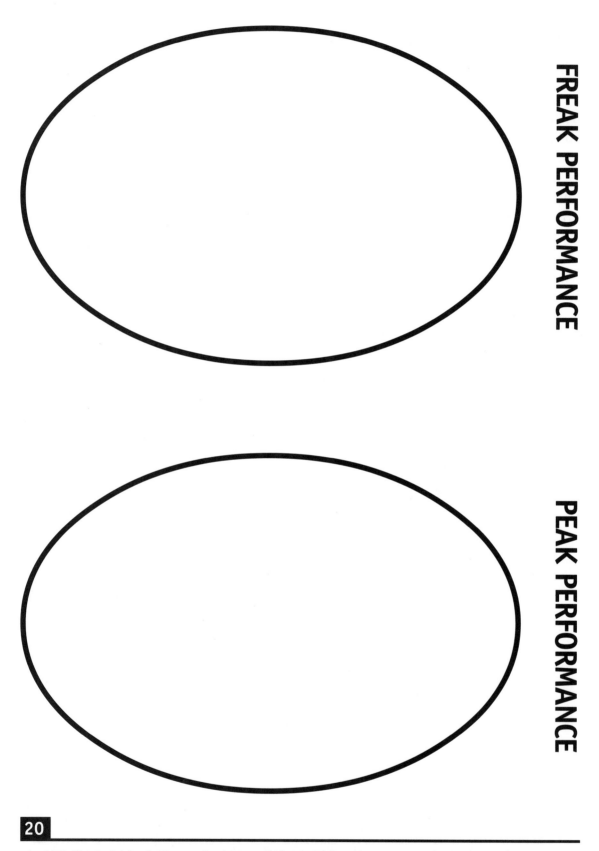

FREAK PERFORMANCE

PEAK PERFORMANCE

20

12. BODY TRACING

Objective
To get your players to recognize and understand the components of peak performance.

Setup
Find a large roll of white or tan roll butcher paper and some magic markers or paint.

Directions
Roll out a large section of the paper and have some of your players lie on top of it in various athletic poses according the positions they play. For example, a baseball and softball team could have players get in positions of a hitter, pitcher, and fielder. Basketball players could either use the guard, forward, and center positions or do a player on offense and one on defense. The Arizona gymnasts did one for each of their four events; vault, bars, beam, and floor. Volleyball could use setters, outside hitters, middle blockers, and defensive specialists.

As they are lying in their athletic poses, instruct a teammate to trace the outline of their body. Cut around the outline with a scissors so that a silhouette of the player is created.

Then players can use their creativity and create the ideal athlete. For example, your players might draw in a strong, pulsating heart signifying the heart of a champion. Or they might draw intense, focused eyes and say that great athletes have the eye of the tiger. Many athletes put words like confidence, or images of success in the athlete's head. In other parts of the body they might show relaxed muscles. Allow your athletes to have some fun with the exercise.

Contributed by:

Laura Kenow
Head Softball Coach
Linfield College

13. MENTAL TOUGHNESS OR MENTAL MORON?

Objective
To get your players to examine things that could mentally get inside their heads and detail plans to overcome them.

Setup
Make copies of the Mental Toughness Response handout for each of your players.

Directions
Ask your players to think about times where they were frustrated, mad, discouraged, or disappointed. Have them list these typical challenging situations in the far left column. Then have them come up with a Mental Moron Response, or a poor way to react to the situation and list it in the far right column.

Then have your athletes look at the same situations and devise a Mental Toughness Response to handle them. This response should help them stay positive and on track mentally or to recover quickly.

For example, an official's poor call is a typical situation which can throw athletes off. The Mental Moron response is to yell and scream at the official and end up getting penalized for it. The Mental Toughness response is the recognize that the official's questionable call is something that is outside of their control. The player should take a deep breath, let it go, and work around and make adjustments to the calls.

Discussion
When your athletes are finished with the exercise, have them cut off the far right column with their Mental Moron responses and throw it away. Then they will only be focused on the challenging situations and their Mental Toughness responses to them. You can have them share their challenging situations and Mental Toughness Responses with their teammates and you may even want to have them practice their responses by acting them out. Also, have your players save the sheet so that they can refer to it often throughout the season.

Adapted from:

David Cook, Ph.D.
Sport Psych Consultant
Mental Advantage, Inc.

mental moron response					

MENTAL TOUGHNESS RESPONSE					

Challenging Situation					

23

14. RED/YELLOW/GREEN LIGHT SKITS

Objective

To get your players to recognize that they can choose how they want to respond to difficult situations and that this choice dictates their success.

Setup

You will need to introduce your players to the mental game traffic light analogy originated by Ken Ravizza and Tom Hanson in their book *Heads Up Baseball*.* Basically, a green light mindset means a player is confident, aggressive, composed, focused, and in control. A yellow light mindset means a player is hesitant, distracted, nervous, and unsure. A red light mindset means a player is angry, frustrated, out of control, feeling helpless, and wanting to give up.

Devise a list of challenging scenarios that your athletes typically must face.
- not getting the playing time they would like
- making a mistake or error during a game
- receiving criticism from a coach or teammate
- getting a poor call from an official
- getting injured or having to sit out for a period of time

Directions

Arrange your players into groups of three people. Hand out one of the scenarios to each of the groups. Using the mental game traffic light analogy, have your players act out a red light response to the situation, a yellow light response, and finally a green light response.

Discussion

How did each of the responses affect the individual's and team's success?
How might a person's response influence a teammate's mental game?
How might a person's response affect an opponent, official, spectator, impressionable child?

Adapted from:

Ken Ravizza & Tom Hanson
Sport Psych Consultants
Authors of Heads Up Baseball
*call (310) 791-0166 to order

15. SECRETS OF SUCCESS SPEAKERS

Objective
To expose your players to success principles in all walks of life and to reinforce what it takes to be successful.

Setup
Invite various performers in approximately once a month to speak with your team about their keys to success. For example, you might want to invite the president of a local bank, an entrepreneur, school board president, surgeon, another successful coach or athlete, etc. to come in and speak with your team.

Discussion
Have your players discuss what this person needed to do to achieve success and how these principles might relate to your team's situation.

Contributed by:

Patrick Murphy
Head Softball Coach
University of Alabama

16. BEST vs. WORST GAME

Objective
To help your players compare and contrast their mindsets during their all-time best and worst games.

Setup
Make copies of the Best vs. Worst Game sheet for all of your players.

Directions
Have your players list their two or three worst all-time games. Ask them to reflect back briefly on the experience in an effort to recall their mindset going into and during the game. Then have your players list their two or three all-time greatest games. Again, have them relive these games in vivid detail and ask them to list how they were thinking before and during the game?

Discussion
What do athletes focus on when they are doing well compared to playing poorly?
How would you describe your confidence level in each of the performances?
What happens to an athlete's body physically as a result of each of the mindsets?
What can athletes do to mentally prepare themselves to consistently perform to their potential?

BEST vs. WORST GAME

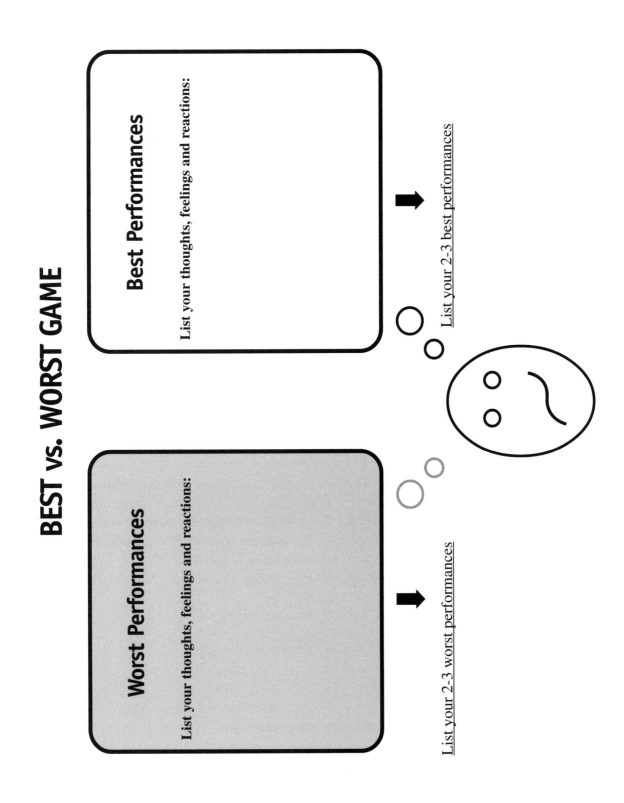

Best Performances

List your thoughts, feelings and reactions:

→ List your 2-3 best performances

Worst Performances

List your thoughts, feelings and reactions:

→ List your 2-3 worst performances

17. GREEN DOTS

Objective

To help your players become more aware of their mental game and take responsibility for creating and maintaining an effective mindset.

Setup

Go to an office supply store such as Staples and purchase a package of green labeling dots. You will also need to introduce your players to the traffic light analogy regarding the mental game (Ravizza & Hanson, 1995)*. A green light mindset means a player is confident, aggressive, composed, focused, and in control. A yellow light mindset means a player is hesitant, distracted, nervous, and unsure. A red light mindset means a player is angry, frustrated, out of control, feeling helpless, and wanting to give up.

Directions

Put the green dots where your players will see them before practicing and performing as a reminder of the importance of having a green light mindset. For example, you can put them on their lockers as a reminder to let go of what happened earlier in the day and to focus 100% on practice. You can put them on the entrance to the gym door or the gate to the field as well. You can put them on their equipment like bats, rackets, clubs, etc. as a reminder to get into the "green" mentally before they perform. Finally, you can put green dots on players shoes, wristbands, etc. as a continual reminder of the importance of having a good mindset when performing.

Coaches, you can also use the green dots to put on your phones at work to remind yourself about the importance of being focused on each conversation. More importantly, put a green dot on the door to your home. This will serve to remind you to let go of the frustrations of the games and practices and to focus on spending quality time with your family and friends.

Analogy adapted from:

Ken Ravizza & Tom Hanson
Sport Psych Consultants
Authors of Heads Up Baseball
call (310) 791-0166 to order

18. STRING AND PAPER CLIP EXERCISE

Objective

To demonstrate to your athletes the power of their thoughts and how they influence the world around them.

Setup

Get a box of large paper clips and a spool of thread or string. Cut the string into strands roughly 20 inches long. Tie one end of the string to paper clip. Also get some small pieces of scrap paper or post-it notes and draw the figure below on them.

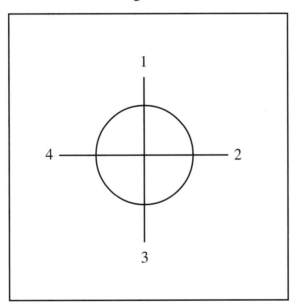

Directions

Tell your players to grab the piece of string between their thumb and forefinger, keeping their wrist somewhat straight yet relaxed. Have them rest their elbow on a table or desk in front of them so that the paper clip dangles roughly one half inch above it. They should then arrange the sheet of paper so that the paper clip hovers over the center of the cross.

Then tell them to begin seeing the paper clip sway up and down between the number one and three, without consciously moving their hands. You can repeat the words "one... three, one... three" and soon most will discover the paper clip to actually begin swaying in the desired direction. Note: Typically 75% of people will be able to get the paper clip to move using their minds. Inform the others that not every person is successful with the first attempt and that this is okay.

Once your athletes have the paper clip swaying in the desired direction for awhile, instruct them to mentally have the paper clip slow down and hover back over the center. Then have them mentally try to make the paper clip sway back in forth between the numbers two and four. Again, allow them some time for this to happen. After going sideways, tell your players to have the paper clip hover over the center again. Now ask your players to have the paper clip move in a clockwise circle around the numbers one, two, three, and four. After completing this, have them then reverse the paper clip in a counter clockwise direction.

Discussion

I had heard of this exercise but had never actually done it until late in my graduate training. Needless to say, I was truly amazed! The exercise is a great one to convince your players about the powers of their minds. It also emphasizes the importance of staying focused on the task at hand.

Primarily, the exercise clearly demonstrates the power of images and how they can affect the environment. The images athletes picture in their minds dictate their performance. What actually happens in the exercise is that by imaging the paper clip to move, the mind sends out a very low, undetectable impulse to the nerves and muscles of the arms and hands. This impulse goes unnoticed by the person but it is enough to make the paper clip move. Thus, you can stress to your athletes that when they visualize performing successfully, they are still training their bodies to perform and enhancing muscle memory.

Adapted from:

Dorothy Harris
Author of The Athlete's Guide to Sport Psychology

19. EXCEEDING YOUR LIMITS

Objective

To demonstrate to your players that they can break through limits and past performances by visualizing future successes and greater levels of achievement.

Directions

Spread your players out and have them stand at least and arm's distance away from each other. Ask them to raise and extend their right arms to chest level with their index fingers pointed straight forward. Then tell them to keep their feet still and to rotate their torsos to their right as far as they can and to note the point by seeing where there index fingers were pointing.

After individually noting how far your players could rotate around, have them close their eyes. Ask them now to visualize doing the same exercise but this time rotating to a point even further around than the first time. Ask them to clearly see this point in the minds, a point that surpasses their first attempt. Have them mentally visualize rotating around and pointing to this point two times.

Then have them open their eyes, outstretch their arms, and rotate to the right once more seeing how far they can go. In most cases, athletes will be able to get to the point they visualized and sometimes even exceed it.

Discussion

This exercise demonstrates to athletes the importance of visualization. It shows them that they can exceed current levels of performance by first visualizing higher levels of performance. Often these improved images are the first steps in helping performers achieve greater levels of success.

20. MENTAL RUBBER BAND

Objective

To demonstrate to your athletes how their minds impact their bodies.

Directions

Have your players clasp their hands together about a foot in front of their faces. Then instruct them to raise and fully extend both index fingers so that they are roughly an inch apart and resemble the number "11". As they gaze at their index fingers, ask them to imagine that there is a very strong rubber band looped around the first knuckles of their fingers. This rubber band is so strong that it feels as if it is pulling their fingers together.

Most athletes will discover that by just imagining a strong rubber band pulling their index fingers together they will indeed actually move closer together.

Discussion

The images in people's minds have a real affect on their bodies. Ask your players what kinds of images they picture in their minds before and after games. Be sure that these images are positive and productive.

PRE-GAME MOTIVATION AND INSPIRATION IDEAS

21. THEMES

Objective

To have your players inspired, focused, and having fun going into games and tournaments. This idea tends to be especially effective when your team (and you) might be uptight about going into the playoffs.

Directions

Sit down with your assistant coaches and/or captains and talk about the current status of your team. Are you the favorite going into the game or the underdog? Has your team been playing well lately or slumping? Are you at full strength or do you have some key players injured? It is important to get a realistic look at the status of your team. Then think about what it will take for your team to be successful. For example, if you are an underdog, you will probably need to believe that your team has a fighting chance for success. In this case you could use the Biblical David and Goliath story, the movie Hoosiers, or the fact that a bumblebee shouldn't be able to fly by aeronautical engineering standards but does anyway.

The key to creating an effective theme is to find an analogy or story which best fits your particular situation. You can then come up with little reminders of the theme to motivate your teams before games and keep them inspired during games.

Examples of Themes

Cross Country Car Race

Present the playoffs as a cross country road race. Each team is symbolized as a car. Emphasize that the best car does not always win the race but the one that is best prepared.

Top Gun Theme - Locked on Target

Talk about playing like a jet fighter squadron. Need to be aggressive and tough while protecting each other. Relate different phases of an attack to various team positions.

Green Berets

Players need to be mentally tough to handle any kind of situation. Green Berets are equipped for guerilla warfare and are good when your team is an underdog with an unconventional way.

Safari - Big Game Hunting

Emphasize that the players need to be in an attack mode and that the law of the jungle is "Survival of the Fittest." Each game is a "big game" and you must hunt down each opponent.

Pirate Theme

Renegade, underdog team looking to steal away a championship from highly-ranked teams.

22. NEWSPAPER ARTICLES

Objective
To get your players thinking and feeling positively heading into a big game.

Setup
Make copies of the Newspaper Articles sheet and arrange your players into pairs with pens/ pencils.

Directions
Tell your players to take turns interviewing each other as if the game already occurred and of course your team was successful. Have the players discuss the keys to success in the game, providing quotes from players, coaches, and even opponents. Make sure each player makes a contribution to the team's success whether it is a starter playing well, a sub coming in and sparking the team, or a reserve enthusiastically cheering on the team to victory.

Discussion
Have your players share their newspaper articles with their teammates. Stress that everyone plays a role with the team and can have a great game even if they don't get playing time. This exercise also gets your players expecting to win and can be used especially when you are the underdog. The important part is to get your players focused on the keys it will take to play well and hopefully get the win.

NEWSPAPER ARTICLES

SPORTS

Hometown Press

headline

Date:

article

picture

caption

50 Drills, Activities & Ideas to Inspire Your Team, Build Mental Toughness & Improve Team Chemistry
© Jeff Janssen • www.jeffjanssen.com • 1-888-721-TEAM

23. HALLIWELL'S HOCKEY STICK

Objective
Halliwell's Hockey Stick is a very powerful pregame motivational tool because it taps into the power of your players' emotions.

Setup
Find a piece of equipment that is often used in your sport. For example, baseball and softball could use a bat, glove, or cleats, basketball could use shoes or a ball, football could use helmets, cleats, or a ball.

Directions
Ask each of your players to think about a person who means a lot to them - someone who has inspired them, who is in the back of their minds each time they take the field. Have your players share who this person is with the rest of the team. Then have the player write the person's name on the equipment you are using. Bring the piece of equipment out and put it by your bench, in your dugout, or on your sideline for the game.

Discussion
This exercise can be a very emotional one for your players so it is best used toward the end of your season or for a major tournament. Typically, emotion brings with it a lot of energy which, if controlled and used properly, can be very effective. It might be best to initiate the exercise the day before the game and then to bring the piece of equipment on game day.

Contributed by:

Wayne Halliwell
Performance Coach
University of Montreal

24. BOUNCE BACK

Objective
To help your team focus on the importance of being resilient, especially after tough losses.

Setup
A tennis ball and an egg (plus a towel for cleanup).

Directions
Assemble your team and hold the tennis ball in one hand and the egg in the other. Drop both. As you catch the tennis ball after it bounces, tell your team that they have one of two options; they can either be like an egg and crack with the adversity, or they can be like the tennis ball and bounce back. It's their choice.

Discussion
Give all your players a tennis ball as a reminder of the exercise and the messages discussed.

Contributed by:

John White
Assistant Principal
Arvada High School (CO)

25. MOTIVATIONAL MOVIES

Objective
Inspirational movies, either in their entirety or more often shown in segments, can have a motivating affect on your team.

Setup
Television, VCR(s), or a video-editing system.

Directions
Have your staff think about the particular situation you are in - be it an underdog trying to win, a team that needs to play more aggressively, or a champion looking to defend your title. After understanding your team's situation, brainstorm some possible movies which center around these circumstances. Then either show your players these movies or you can splice clips from the movies into your tapes.

Discussion
Be sure that your players understand the underlying message of the motivational movie.

Examples of Motivational Movies:

Hoosiers
Rudy
Braveheart
Rocky
Chariots of Fire
Remember the Titans

DRILLS TO SHARPEN FOCUS

26. CONCENTRATION GRID EXERCISE

Objective

The objective of this challenging and fun exercise is to teach your athletes the importance of focused concentration as well as what can happen to a person's focus under stress.

Setup

Make copies of the Concentration Grid sheet and provide your athletes with pens or pencils.

Directions

Tell your players that you will be testing their focus using the Concentration Grid. Every number from 0 to 99 is randomly located somewhere on the 10 by 10 grid.

The players will be asked to begin by searching for a specific number of your choosing, such as the number 23. The players may search the grid however they want. Upon finding the specified number (23), players should put a slash through it. Then they need to search for the next consecutive number (24). Upon finding the next number players should slash it as well. This process continues for one minute. After this time, players should count up the total number of slashes (numbers) they were able to get.

This exercise can easily be made competitive by asking players to compare scores. Typically high scores range between 15-20 when given one minute to complete the exercise.

The exercise can be made even more competitive by pairing teammates up with a partner. While one person attempts to complete the exercise, their partner is allowed to distract them verbally by saying other random numbers, telling jokes, singing, talking trash, etc. Be sure to remind the distractors that they may only use verbal distractions and are not allowed to touch their partner's body, paper, or pen, or block their vision in any way. Go through the exercise twice with distractions so each person gets a turn in each role.

Discussion

In addition to being a lot of fun for your players, this exercise creates several topics for discussion. Talk with your players about their stress levels when they struggled finding numbers.

Ask them about the mental strategies they used to focus on the numbers. Did they say the numbers to themselves using their self-talk, have an image of the number, or use a combination of the two? Whatever strategy they used can be transferred to the sporting world.

If you used distractors, compare players' scores with distractions to silence. Typically, two out of three people will do worse with distractions. However, one third will actually improve with distractions. You can ask those who improved which mental strategies they used. Finally this exercise can be used regularly to train and enhance concentration skills.

CONCENTRATION GRID EXERCISE

63	84	12	24	28	27	19	83	40	32
60	51	25	45	20	02	76	96	72	78
37	91	56	66	36	48	87	65	04	59
16	30	41	14	69	34	44	82	71	39
97	52	23	38	15	58	94	62	00	53
67	89	95	80	90	13	21	08	26	74
92	42	88	70	06	79	93	47	98	77
31	85	73	64	75	54	43	10	46	18
33	50	68	05	11	35	81	49	57	61
03	09	99	22	07	17	01	86	29	55

13	21	08	26	74	67	89	95	80	90
79	93	47	98	77	92	42	88	70	06
54	43	10	46	18	31	85	73	64	75
35	81	49	57	61	33	50	68	05	11
17	01	86	29	55	03	09	99	22	07
27	19	83	40	32	63	84	12	24	28
02	76	96	72	78	60	51	25	45	20
48	87	65	04	59	37	91	56	66	36
34	44	82	71	39	16	30	41	14	69
58	94	62	00	53	97	52	23	38	15

50 Drills, Activities & Ideas to Inspire Your Team, Build Mental Toughness & Improve Team Chemistry
© Jeff Janssen • www.jeffjanssen.com • 1-888-721-TEAM

27. THE PICKLE JAR

Objective

To help your players recognize and release negative thoughts prior to a practice or competition.

Setup

An empty pickle or other small to medium sized jar, pens or pencils, and pieces of scrap paper.

Directions

As players begin showing up for practice, hand each of them a piece of scrap paper and a pen. Ask them to think about all the things that might be on their minds as they come to practice. These could be problems that occurred earlier in the day, being in a bad mood, worries about future exams, projects, or concerns about finances, friends, etc. Tell your players to list all of these concerns on their piece of scrap paper.

Then have your players fold the sheets of paper so that they can fit into the pickle jar. Once all the papers listing the players problems and worries are in the jar, seal it tightly.

Discussion

Help your players understand that focusing on these problems and concerns during your practice time is a very unproductive use of their time. Obviously, players will have things on their minds when they come to practice. However, to have a quality practice where players are focused, it is important that they set aside their other concerns during practice time. Of course, once practice is over they can always take the sheet out of the jar and continue to worry about these concerns if they so choose.

Similarly, this exercise can be used by players following practice so that their minds may be clear and focused for studying or social time as well.

Note: Obviously, in a few instances during the season your players may arrive at practice in a distracted or emotional state because of some serious problems or concerns. It is often wise to take these players aside and talk with them and/or give them a day off in an effort to help them cope with this kind of more serious situation.

28. TAKING CARE OF THE PROCESS

Objective

To focus your players on the simple, controllable, little things that they can do to achieve the goals and outcomes they want. It is a great way to break down a big game and big goals into more manageable chunks.

Setup

Copies of the Taking Care of the Process sheets for your players and pens/pencils.

Directions

Have your players list some of the goals they are striving for such as being a starter, averaging 15+ points a game, pitching a shutout, or returning in full form from an injury. Then have them list three to five of the most important things they can do which will make the outcome they want much more likely to happen.

For example, if a player wants to average 15+ points a game, they will need to focus on developing their one on one moves, using screens effectively, making at least 80% of their free throws, getting easy baskets off transition, and hitting the offensive boards for put-backs.

A pitcher who wants to pitch a shutout should focus on having a great command of the strike zone, working on her spins to get her pitches to move, increasing her speed through long toss, perfecting her changeup to get players off balance, and working with her catcher to study the hitters so that they can pitch to the hitters' weaknesses.

Finally, in his book *Faith in the Game,* former Nebraska football coach Tom Osborne outlined process goals for the offense, defense, and special teams. Some of these goals included averaging six or more yards per rush, one or no turnovers per game, hold opponents to three yards or less per rush, hold opponents under 13 points, and no blocked kicks.

Discussion

The important part of this exercise is to shift your players focus from outcomes that may seem difficult, overwhelming, and out of their control, to concentrating on simple things that they can control that will dramatically increase the odds of getting the outcomes they desire.

Your players should focus on these process factors before the game and focus their energies and goals in these areas. Further, during breaks in the game, you can use these three to five areas as checkpoints to keep your players focused on the process and quickly evaluate their progress. Finally, the process factors provide a great way to evaluate a competition outside of just winning or losing. When players fail to achieve the outcomes they want, it is most often because they did not take care of the process goals.

TAKING CARE OF THE PROCESS

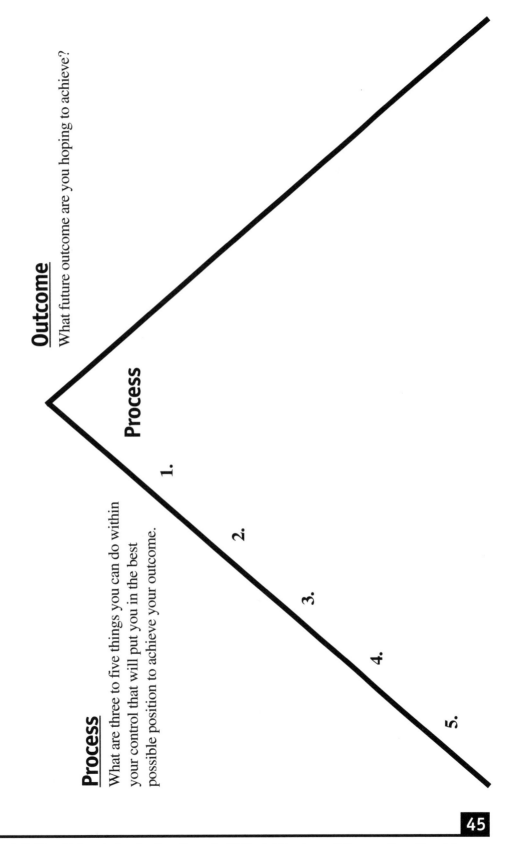

Outcome
What future outcome are you hoping to achieve?

Process

1.

2.

3.

4.

5.

Process
What are three to five things you can do within your control that will put you in the best possible position to achieve your outcome.

29. CONTROLLABLES CHALLENGE

Objective

To help your players recognize and focus on the things they can control as they practice and play rather than the things they cannot.

Setup

Make copies of the Controlling the Controllables sheet.

Directions

If you have a small number of players on you team (10 or less) you can do this individually. However, if you have more than 10 players it is often better to get them into teams of two or three people.

Ask your players to think about all the things which could affect them when they perform but they have little to no control over. These things could include officials, weather, playing conditions, playing time, etc. Have each player/group attempt to list as many general categories of things they cannot control in the outer gray octagon. Allow your players roughly three minutes to do this. Tell them they are trying to get as many general categories as possible within the specified time limit. (For example, by general categories I mean "umpires" would include both the home plate umpire and any base umpire. As a coach, you are the final judge on whether answers overlap.)

Once the specified time limit is up, go around to each group and have them report one of their responses. As long as the team can provide an answer which is an uncontrollable, as agreed upon by the other groups and coach, the group stays in the game. The other groups then should check their sheets and cross off any answer which matches or closely approximates one they have on their sheets. This process continues in an elimination round type fashion until the groups have exhausted all of their answers. The last group to give a response is the winner.

Discussion

It is important for athletes to recognize the multitude of factors which are outside of their control when they compete. Remind them that focusing on these things and using them as excuses only makes the situation worse - hence the stop sign shape is used for the uncontrollables. However, when they focus on the things they can control, athletes have a much better chance of keeping composed and being successful.

CONTROLLABLES CHALLENGE

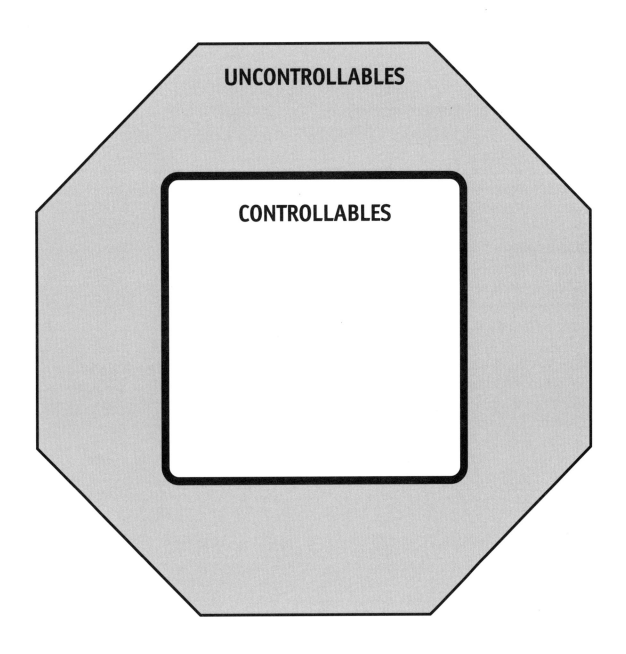

UNCONTROLLABLES

CONTROLLABLES

30. SQUIRT BOTTLE DISTRACTION

Objective
To train athletes to stay focused on the task at hand despite being distracted by squirts of water.

Setup
Fill an old, clean squirt bottle with water.

Directions
As an athlete is practicing a skill, stand near him with a squirt bottle. At random intervals squirt the player with a stream of water to see if he can maintain his composure and concentration.

Discussion
How well did the person respond to the distraction?
Did the athlete have any control over the distraction?
What are other examples of distractions that athletes must face?
What did the athlete focus on to successful overcome the distraction?

Note: You can also attempt to distract your players through distracting sounds or noises. College football teams have been known to blare the fight songs of opponents during practices over and over again to see how their players handle the adversity. Additionally, some coaches have run leaf blowers on the sidelines to create noise and to see if their players can still call plays and audibles effectively.

EXERCISES TO BUILD CONFIDENCE

31. REASONS WE DESERVE SUCCESS

Objective
To help your players focus on all the reasons why they should be confident going into a game or tournament.

Setup
Sheets of lined paper and pens/pencils.

Directions
Assemble your players into three different groups. Ask them to brainstorm and list all the reasons they should be confident. Ask them about what drills they have done, past successes they might have had, their team strengths, and any compliments they have received. After giving the groups five minutes to brainstorm their answers, have the groups give responses from their list one at a time. Be sure to list all the reasons on the board.

Discussion
Remind your players that confidence is something that is first earned through quality preparation, and then chosen by focusing on all the things you have going for you. After the groups have listed all the reasons, make a copy of the list, post it in the locker room, and distribute a copy to each player.

50 Drills, Activities & Ideas to Inspire Your Team, Build Mental Toughness & Improve Team Chemistry
© Jeff Janssen • www.jeffjanssen.com • 1-888-721-TEAM

32. SCOUTING REPORT

Objective
To build your player's confidence and get them to focus on what they do well rather than their opponent's strengths.

Setup
This idea is especially good when your team is the underdog and might be a bit intimidated going into the game.

Directions
Most scouting reports generally focus on the other team's personnel, plays, and strengths. However, in this scouting report, you actually discuss your own team's strengths. For example, list your own players and highlight their strengths. Talk about the things you do well and plan to execute in the game. Get so hyped up about your players' strengths that it doesn't even matter who the other team is. Help your players believe in themselves.

Discussion
While it is good to know your opponent's strengths and tendencies, be sure that your players know their own, especially when you are facing tough competition. Too often players have a tendency to put formidable opponents up on a pedestal. When you see opponents as stronger and better than you, you have little chance for success. However, when you build your players up by focusing on their strengths, you demonstrate your confidence in them.

33. SUCCESS AUDIOTAPES

Objective
To build and focus on creating confidence before practices and competition. Success audio-tapes also program a player's mind to think effectively and expect success.

Setup
Cassette recorder, boom box, blank audio tape, and script.

Directions
1. Have your players think about their goals for an upcoming competition and imagine what it would be like to achieve them. Have them write a script detailing exactly the way they would like to play from their warm-up time all the way through the end of the game.
Some possible things players could include in the script:
   • Their physical and mental strengths (great shooter, good leader, enthusiastic)
   • Any past successes they might have had (won last race, good practices)
   • What they like about the field/court (home crowd, away crowd motivates you)
   • Their pre-performance thoughts and feelings (confident, relaxed, ready)
   • Thoughts they have when performing well (automatic, unstoppable, in control)
   • Create a cue word that describes a successful mindset (trust, dominate, going all out)
   • Things they need to do to be successful (strategy, key points, attitude)
   • All of their senses (sights, sounds, movements, feelings, etc.)
   • A mental play-by-play of key moments (start, offense/defense, adversity, end of game)

2. Use first person statements for the script - "I feel..., I am...,"
3. Make the script as creative and as real as possible.
4. Read the script on to a tape with expression and background music that sets the tone of how the player wants to feel. Keep the tape short (3-5 min.) so it is easy to listen to.
5. Once the Success Audiotape is created, players should listen to it regularly (at least once a day). The player should seek to visualize and experience the tape, not just listen to it.

Adapted from:

David Cook, Ph.D.
Sport Psych Consultant
Mental Advantage, Inc.

34. HIGHLIGHT VIDEOS

Objective
To motivate your players and remind them of past successes so they can build their confidence and sharpen their focus.

Setup
Video editing system or two VCRs hooked together (see VCR instruction manual).

Directions
Much like ESPN, find video clips where your team is playing well, having fun, being mentally tough, or performing well as a team. Compile these clips with some inspiring music in the background. Then play the tape the day before a big game or the morning of the game.

Discussion
The University of Arizona softball team creates a highlight video each season before NCAA Regionals. The team gets together to watch the tape before every playoff game. As the team advances, new clips and songs are added.

35. WHIPPED CREAM CHALLENGE

Objective
To test your player's confidence, have some fun, and add some spice (or shall I say sugar?) to practice.

Setup
A canister of spray-on whipped cream.

Directions
Allow your players to challenge each other to execute a skill in a pressure-packed situation. For example, one player may challenge another to make two free throws while the entire team is trying to distract her in the background. If the player misses, the challenger gets to smear whipped cream in the shooter's face. However, if the challengee successful executes the challenge, the challenger must suffer the whipped cream consequences. Challengers and challengees must mutually agree to the challenge. They also must be willing to undergo the punishment if they lose.

Discussion
Obviously, this activity is best done at the end of practice because things can get silly in a hurry. However, the activity is a good way to see if a player can be composed and confident under pressure. It also is a great way to add some fun to a practice.

Discuss how the whipped cream challenge either helped or hindered your players focus, confidence, and motivation.

IDEAS FOR ENHANCING MOTIVATION AND COMMITMENT

36. GOAL DARES

Objective

To help your players practice with a purpose as well as provide them with the motivation to improve.

Directions

Pair up your players. Have each player then draft a goal that can easily be measured and verified by the end of the week. Also, be sure that the goal is realistic yet challenging at the same time. It's the partner's job to make sure the goal is challenging because the partner will owe the other person something if the person achieves the goal. Or the person setting the goal may owe their partner something if the person doesn't achieve their goal.

For example, a person may set a goal of making 7 out of 10 free throws after practice. After showing the drafted goal to their partner, the partner insists it be 8 out of 10 because the person is a 75% free throw shooter. If the person makes the 8 out of 10 the partner will agree to buy him a hot fudge sundae at the end of the week.

Or a softball player could dare her partner to get 4 out of 5 bunts down in fair territory during a drill. If the person fails to get four or more bunts down, her partner will carry her bat bag to and from practice for one week.

Discussion

Goal dares add a little fun and incentive to practices because something is riding on the outcome of drills. Coaches can occasionally dare players to achieve certain goals as well (of course be careful about NCAA rules).

37. TEAM QUOTES

Objective

To share the responsibility of team motivation with your players and allow them the chance to find and read inspirational quotes that mean a lot to them.

Setup

Bulletin board, thumb tacks, and paper.

Directions

Assign one player to bring in one or more inspirational quotes for a day or week of practice. Have the player read the quote to the team and explain why they chose the quote and what it means to them. Tack the quote on the bulletin board. You can have players bring in quotes on a daily or weekly basis.

Here is a list of some books where you and your players can find some great quotes:

The Edge by Howard Ferguson
Winning by Michael Lynberg
Get Motivated!: Daily Psych-ups by Kara Leverte Farley & Sheila M. Curry
The Olympians' Guide to Winning the Game of Life by Bud Greenspan
The Coaches' Little Playbook by George Hetzel, Jr.
The Best of Success by Wynn Davis
Winning Words of Champions by Larry Bielat

38. STUCK ON STICKERS

Objective
To provide an incentive for your players to achieve certain levels of performance.

Setup
Pre-made or custom stickers to stick on a board or on equipment such as helmets.

Directions
Determine exemplary levels of performance for all phases of your game. For example, 10+ rebounds, one or two charges taken, 8+ assists, 80%+ free throw percentage, three or more blocked shots, 5+ steals, etc. If a player achieves this level of performance, they will be awarded a sticker on a chart.

Discussion
This incentive system can work well for your starters but you need to get a little more creative for your substitutes. For example, University of Arizona softball coach Mike Candrea awards our pinch-runners with stickers each time they score.

39. PERFORMANCE CLUBS

Objective
To provide your players with an incentive to practice during the off season.

Setup
Some type of imprinted clothing item or other award for prospective club members.

Directions
Think about how much you would realistically like your players to practice on a daily basis during their off season. For example, a basketball coach might wish her players would shoot 200 shots a day, 5 days a week during the off season. At this rate the player would have 1,000 shots each week.

Multiply this number by the number of weeks in the off season with the consideration of allowing them some time to relax and recuperate. Let's say there are roughly 10 available weeks during your off season. Thus the goal would be to shoot 10,000 shots in the off season. Players achieving this level would be awarded a shirt saying the "10,000 Shot Club."

Tell your players that the ones who successfully accomplish this off-season program will be awarded with the "10,000 Shot Club" t-shirt when they return. Have your players send you their number of shots on a weekly basis to promote accountability. Ultimately, they are on the honor system to be honest but the shirt does serve as an incentive and promotes pride in working hard during off-season workouts.

Contributed by:

John White
Assistant Principal
Arvada High School (CO)

40. PICTURING SUCCESS POSTER

Objective
To help your players create concrete mental pictures of their future goals and dreams. The poster also serves as a continual reminder of the player's mission, especially when they might be struggling.

Setup
Pieces of poster board, glue sticks/tape, old (sport) magazines and newspapers, markers.

Directions
Ask your players to look through old magazines and sports pages to find any pictures, phrases, or words that depict the kind of player they want to be and the goals they want to achieve. Have them cut out the images and words and glue them to the poster board in a creative way. The players can also write or draw things on their poster boards if they cannot locate the ideal picture they want.

Discussion
Have the players describe their completed posters with their teammates. Then have the player put up the poster somewhere they will see it on a daily basis - by their locker, in their bedrooms, etc.

STRATEGIES FOR MAKING PRACTICES FUN AND EFFECTIVE

41. ROVING PRACTICE SHIRT

Objective
To provide your players with an incentive to work hard in practices.

Setup
Create a special shirt or jersey that might say something like "Practice Player of the Week."

Directions
Remind your players that their effort and performance in practice is the key to the team's success. In an effort to emphasize how important practice performance is, you have created a special award signified by the jersey. At the end of the week of practice, the players are to vote for the person (excluding themselves) who they think gave the best effort in practice. This person then gets to wear the jersey for the following week of practice.

Discussion
Be sure to remind your players that this is not a popularity contest but that they should vote for the player who deserves the honor. In the case of a tie, the coach should cast the deciding vote. It is also wise to honorably mention and acknowledge the players who received several, but not the most votes.

42. QUALITY PRACTICE REWARDS

Objective
To encourage your players to bring a productive attitude and get the most out of practice.

Setup
Boom box stereo and/or sound system, popsicles, popcorn, Kudos candy bars, etc.

Directions
Store up some kind of reward type items such as popsicles on hot summer days, popcorn for film sessions, Kudos candy bars for a job well done, and music to be played at practices. Then, a few select times during the season, when your players have especially good practices, acknowledge and reward them with one of the mentioned items. Your players will really appreciate the special perks and you will reinforce the importance of quality practices.

Discussion
Give the special rewards only occasionally so as your players will not come to expect them every time they practice well. You want your players to practice hard for the intrinsic rewards and benefits, not because they will get something for it.

43. TRANSITION SYMBOLS

Objective

To help your players make the mental transition from being a student during the day to becoming an athlete in time for practice. The purpose is to get players to let go of any distractions or stresses they might have and to focus fully on getting the most out of practices.

Setup

Logo, slogan, or sign in sheet.

Directions

Remind your players about the importance of being 100% focused on practices and workouts during the limited time that you have. Acknowledge that there are obviously a lot of things that could be on their minds, but that it is important that they let them go and be mentally prepared for practice.

Ask them if there are any ideas that they might have to help themselves make the mental transition from what went on earlier in the day to now focusing on practices. Some teams use things associated with the field such as walking through the gates signifies a player is 100% ready to practice. Some players use the transition time in the locker room when they change clothes. When they take off their street clothes, it signals them to let go of their outside thoughts. As they put on their practice clothes it reminds them to get into the athlete mode.

Some teams use logos and sayings on walls that athletes touch every time they leave the locker room before heading out to the field/court. Other coaches have their players sign-in during stretching to show that the player is both physically and mentally present.

Whatever the case, ask your players to create some kind of symbol or cue that they will use which will remind them to let go of distracting thoughts and focus totally on being a successful athlete during your practice time.

Additionally, encourage your players to either use the same or different symbol to let go of practices when they are finished so that they can focus on studying and the rest of their day.

44. CROSS TRAINING CHALLENGES

Objective
To break up the monotony of practice, have some fun, build team chemistry, and still get a good workout.

Setup
Frisbees, floor hockey sticks and goals, a swimming pool, dodge balls, Nerf football, etc.

Directions
As a coach, you will have a feel for your team as to when is the best time for initiating these games. Typically, a great time is after a tough loss or series of losses and you want to emphasize the importance of having some fun.

Instead of practicing your sport, arrange your players into teams and let them play a competitive activity unrelated to your sport. For example, you could have your team play a game of Nerf or frisbee football. If you are a basketball coach, check with the P.E. teacher to see if they might have some floor hockey sticks for a game. Arizona's football team typically has a swim meet during their preseason training camp to add some fun.

These games bring out the fun and competitive nature in everyone and are a great way to mentally rejuvenate your players.

Discussion
Talk with your players about their mental approaches in these games. Were there any things that they did during these games that they need to remember to apply to their sport?

45. PHANTOM DRILLS

Objective
To break up the monotony of practice and encourage your players to stretch their imaginations as to what is possible.

Directions
This exercise uses pure imagination. Using softball/baseball as an example, coaches and players go through an imaginary pregame infield warm-up as if they actually are playing - however there is no ball involved. Coaches hit imaginary fungos to players who make spectacular plays in the field.

Similarly, other sports can run flawlessly through their plays without a ball, making spectacular plays as they go. While it might look strange to the casual observer, the players are setting themselves up for success.

Contributed by:

Lu Harris
Head Softball Coach
Univeristy of Georgia

EXERCISES FOR CONSTRUCTIVE EVALUATION

50 Drills, Activities & Ideas to Inspire Your Team, Build Mental Toughness & Improve Team Chemistry
© Jeff Janssen • www.jeffjanssen.com • 1-888-721-TEAM

46. HIGHLIGHTS AND LESSONS

Objective

To help your players constructively evaluate a game or week of practice.

Setup

Copies of the Highlights and Lessons sheet.

Directions

This exercise can be used effectively to evaluate a game or week of practice. About a day after the game, hand out the sheet to your players. Ask them to go back and think about any individual or team great plays that they can remember. Have them describe the plays in the highlight section. Then, ask them to recall any mistakes the team might have made. Instead of having them list the mistake, have them list the lessons they learned and the adjustment they plan to make the next time the situation arises.

After your players do this on their own, ask them to share some of the highlights they saw in an effort to build confidence. Then have them discuss the lessons the team learned. This process can and should be done following both wins and losses. It is important to realize that there are some highlights during losses just as their are things that can be modified and improved after wins.

Discussion

Too often, players relive only the mistakes they made, playing them over and over again in their minds. It's no wonder that they often dwell on the problems. This exercise encourages your players to find the positives so that they can build confidence. It also transforms any mistakes they might have made into future lessons and eventual successes.

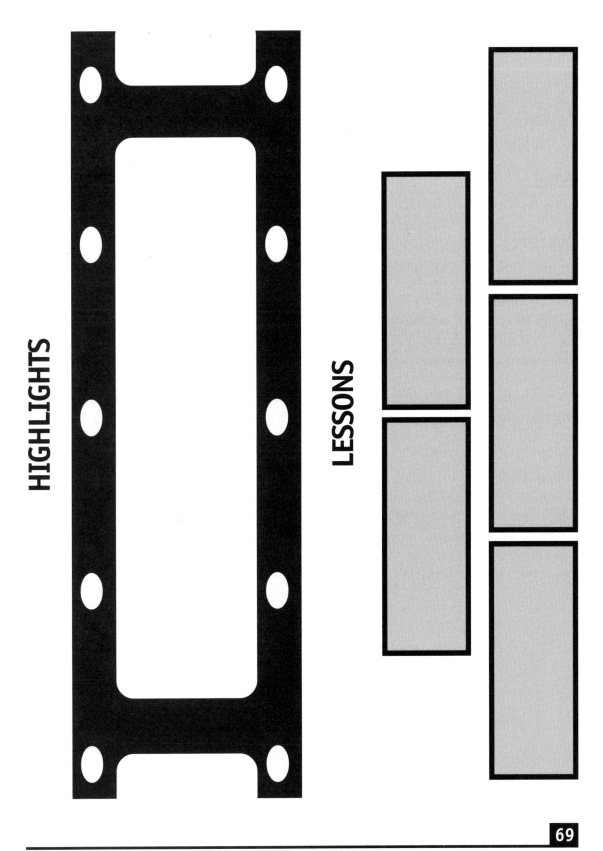

HIGHLIGHTS

LESSONS

47. MENTAL GAME EVALUATION

Objective
To help your players evaluate a game from a mental standpoint.

Setup
Three copies of the Mental Game Evaluation sheet, pens/pencils.

Directions
Arrange your players into three different groups. Hand out one of the Mental Game Evaluation sheets to each group. Have the group think of some of the key points during the game - the start, times when the momentum might have swung, times when your team was on a roll, times when the team was floundering and struggling, etc.

Have your players discuss how effective (terrible through great) the team's mental game was during these key times and to plot it accordingly on the graph. After the players have plotted various points in relation to where their mental game was at specific points during the game, have them connect the dots. Then they should draw their plots and line up on a white board or chalkboard. Have the other two groups do the same. Then each group should explain their charts.

Discussion
Be sure to focus on the times when the team's mental game was going well. Try to determine what exactly it was that helped the team be in a good mental state. Then look at the areas where the graph starts to go down. Determine what happened and why the graph went down. Also, focus on the areas where the graph angles upward and figure out what was done to swing the momentum back in the team's favor.

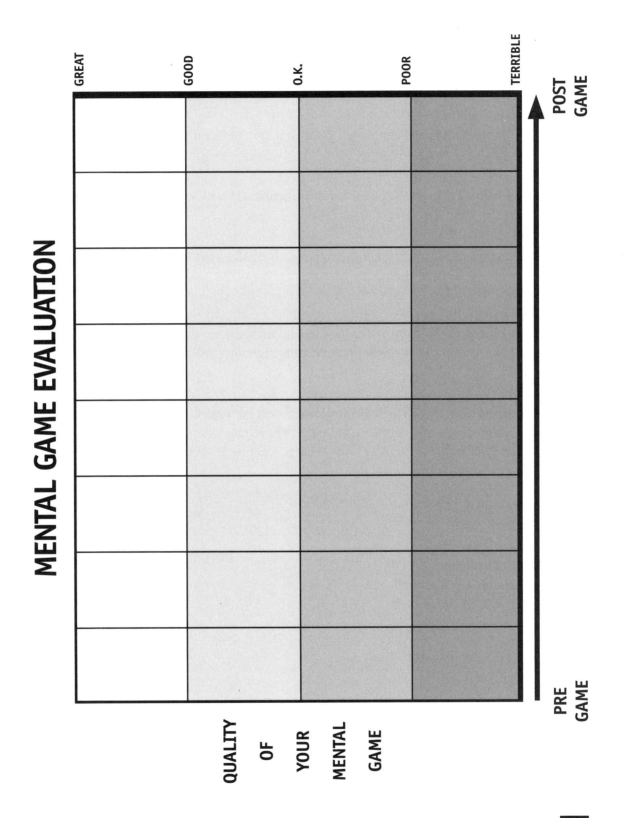

MENTAL GAME EVALUATION

GREAT
GOOD
O.K.
POOR
TERRIBLE

POST GAME

PRE GAME

QUALITY OF YOUR MENTAL GAME

48. TRAFFIC LIGHT EVALUATION

Objective
To have your players evaluate their mental game in relation to their performance.

Setup
Copies of the Traffic Light Evaluation sheet, pens/pencils. Have your players find a partner.

Directions
Using Ken Ravizza's traffic light analogy from *Heads Up Baseball** (see page 25), have your players interview each other to examine what percentage of the game they felt they were in each color light. For the green light section, the players should interview their partners to find out what percentage of the game the person was thinking effectively, what segments of the game the person was in the green, and what they did mentally to create an effective mindset. Similarly, the players should interview their partners regarding yellow and red light situations.

Discussion
Have your players discuss with their partners how much their mental game affected their performances. After each of your individual players have rated themselves you can apply the exercise to the team's mental game. Discuss what percentage of the time your players felt the team was in a green, yellow, and red.

Analogy adapted from:

Ken Ravizza & Tom Hanson
Sport Psych Consultants
Authors of Heads Up Baseball
**call (310) 791-0166 to order*

TRAFFIC LIGHT EVALUATION

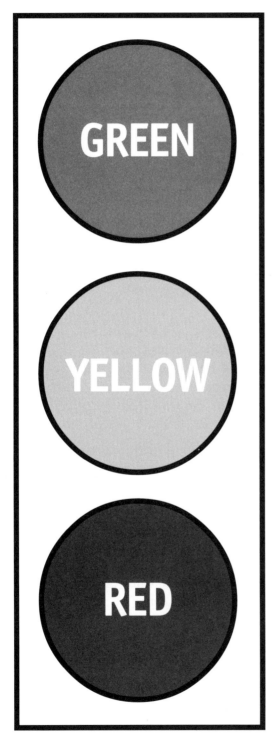

When were you in the green?   % of game

What did you do to get in the green?

When were you in the yellow?   % of game

How did/could you get back to green?

When were you in the red?   % of game

How will you prevent the red from happening next time?

49. LUTE'S TOP THREE

Objective

To get your player's input and insights on the best and weakest players on your team.

Setup

Depending on your sport, create a Player Evaluation sheet similar to the one below.

Directions

Hand out the Player Evaluation sheet to your players. Ask them to privately answer each question as honestly as possible. Once they return them to you, tally and rank all the responses and share them with your coaching staff.

PLAYER EVALUATION

List the 3 best rebounders.	List the 3 weakest rebounders.
List the 3 best defenders.	List the 3 weakest defenders.
List the 3 best passers.	List the 3 weakest passers.
List the 3 best team attitudes.	List the 3 poorest team attitudes.
List the 3 most intense players.	List the 3 laziest players.

If you were a starter, list the other players you would want to start with you:

Which player(s) do you most often look to for leadership?

Which player(s) would you want to take the shot with the game on the line?

Discussion

This exercise gives you some insight on how your players view each other. If done honestly, it will probably confirm what you already know, but it usually gives you an new insight as well. It is best to keep the information from this evaluation within your coaching staff. However, the information from this evaluation has been used by coaches to substantiate and justify why a player may not be getting playing time. Certain players may not agree with your assessments of them but if their teammates are all saying it as well, it is much harder to refute.

Contributed by:

Lute Olson and Jim Rosborough
Arizona Men's Basketball
NCAA National Champions 1997

50. BOOK OF THE MONTH/YEAR CLUB

Objective
To help your players evaluate the success principles of other great athletes and coaches. By reading and discussing various sections and chapters, your players will begin to understand what it takes to be successful and apply the lessons to their games.

Directions
Select a book or article containing several messages you would like your players to adopt. It is also a good idea to select a book by a person who plays the same sport or your players can relate to.

For example, Coach John White, formerly of Dakota Ridge High School, the 1999 4A Colorado State Champions, selected Rick Pitino's book *Success is a Choice*. Penn State women's basketball read Pat Summitt's *Reach for the Summit*. Then you can assign your players to read a certain amount of chapters on a weekly or monthly basis.

Michael Johnson - *Slaying the Dragon*
Pat Riley - *The Winner Within*
Michael Jordan - *I Can't Accept Not Trying*
Dennis Connor - *The Art of Winning*
Mia Hamm - *Go for the Goal*
Dot Richardson - *Living the Dream*

Discussion
Obviously, the content of the book will provide the primary basis for your discussion. You can either take the lead and generate the discussion with your comments and questions. Or you can assign one or two players to take the lead for certain chapters.

Contributed by:

John White
Assistant Principal
Arvada High School (CO)

ABOUT JEFF JANSSEN, M.S.

As one the nation's premiere Peak Performance Coaches, Jeff Janssen, M.S. helps sport and business teams develop the mental toughness and team chemistry necessary to perform to their potential. As a consultant to many of the nation's top colleges including Stanford, Tennessee, Florida, Florida State, Colorado, Iowa State, Wisconsin, Alabama, LSU, and Arizona, Janssen's work has contributed to numerous NCAA National Championships and Final Four appearances across a variety of sports. A popular and frequent speaker at schools and coaches clinics across the nation, Jeff has presented over 750 programs on peak performance, team building, and leadership.

In addition to the sporting world, Jeff speaks to and consults with Fortune 500 companies including Federal Express, Raytheon, and New York Life. Janssen's interactive and inspiring workshops provide businesses with the important mental edge in the competitive corporate arena.

As a result of his work and experience with elite athletes and leaders, Janssen has written and produced several books, articles, audios, and videos on peak performance, team building, and credible coaching. His groundbreaking books *Championship Team Building* and *The Seven Secrets of Successful Coaches* have received rave reviews from coaches and business managers alike.

Jeff resides in Cary, North Carolina with his wife Kristi, son Ryan, and daughter Jill. They enjoy hiking, traveling, reading, and playing sports.

How to Contribute to Future Volumes of the Peak Performance Playbook

If you have any drills, activities, or ideas that you would like to contribute to future volumes of the Playbook, please e-mail them to me at jeff@jeffjanssen.com. If I include your idea in the Playbook I will credit you as the source and send you a complimentary copy when it becomes available.

Peak Performance Programs Available

Need some help in designing a team building workshop or retreat for your team/staff? Jeff offers Peak Performance workshops designed to help you incorporate team building and mental game drills into your training. E-mail Jeff at jeff@jeffjanssen.com or call 1-888-721-TEAM for more information on his consulting packages.

PEAK PERFORMANCE PROGRAMS

Gain the mental edge, build great team chemistry, become a more credible coach, and develop responsible and respected team leaders with Jeff Janssen's Peak Performance Programs.

Peak Performance Seminar

This innovative and interactive seminar shows coaches and athletes how to Master The Mental Game for success in sport, school, and the game of life. You and your team will learn how to effectively build your confidence, sharpen your focus, perform under pressure, trust your talents, overcome obstacles and adversity, and become more mentally tough. Thousands of professional, collegiate, and high school athletes across the nation have gained the mental advantage through this powerful and inspiring seminar.

Championship Team Building Workshop

Based on Jeff's popular book *Championship Team Building*, this customized team building workshop gives you and your team the insights and strategies necessary to develop great team chemistry. The fun and fast-paced workshop uses several team building games, challenges, and exercises to reveal the strengths and areas for improvement of your team. Determine a common and compelling goal, build a lasting commitment, define and appreciate roles, communicate more clearly, minimize and manage conflict, and create a more cohesive team. This workshop can also be adapted for coaches who want to learn more about team building.

The Seven Secrets of Successful Coaches™ Workshop

This coaches' development workshop reveals The Seven Secrets of Successful Coaches™ and gives you the skills to unlock and unleash you team's full potential. Learn how to communicate more effectively with your athletes, build their confidence and commitment, handle difficult players and discipline, motivate and inspire your team, earn your athletes' respect, and leave a lasting legacy as a coach. Makes an ideal continuing education program for your college or high school athletic department coaching staff.

Developing Responsible and Respected Team Captains/Leaders Workshop

This leadership workshop is ideal for college and high school athletic departments who want to develop dynamic, responsible, and effective leaders both in sport and the game of life. Create leaders who will set and maintain high standards, promote a respectful, responsible, and accountable environment, combat negativity and complacency, constructively confront undisciplined teammates, and keep your team focused when adversity strikes. Help your program develop the positive and powerful leaders it needs to win.

As one of the nation's premiere Peak Performance Coaches, Jeff Janssen, M.S. helps coaches and athletes develop the team chemistry, mental toughness, and leadership skills necessary to win championships. Janssen has presented programs at Tennessee, Stanford, Texas, Colorado, Purdue, North Carolina State, Florida, Arizona, Maryland, Florida State, Iowa State, and dozens of other colleges. His work has contributed to numerous NCAA National Championships and Final Fours. He is the author of two ground breaking books *Championship Team Building* and *The Seven Secrets of Successful Coaches*.

Presentation Rates and Fees

Call 1-888-721-TEAM for more information on Jeff's programs, fees, and availability.
NCAA Schools: The NCAA offers a $500 Sport Sciences Speakers Grant to help offset your costs.

JANSSEN
Peak Performance
6841 Piershill Lane
Cary, NC 27519

Jeff Janssen, M.S.
1-888-721-TEAM
jeff@jeffjanssen.com
www.jeffjanssen.com

"Practical and Proven Ideas to Help You Perform to Your Potential"

Perform to Your Potential with Jeff Janssen's Peak Performance Products

● **CHAMPIONSHIP TEAM BUILDING book**
  What Every Coach Needs to Know to Build a Motivated, Committed & Cohesive Team
  This groundbreaking book details dozens of proven strategies to help you develop great team chemistry. Discover the Seven "C's" of Championship Team Building. Solve the problems that could distract, divide, and destroy your team. Includes 38 team building drills. $29.95, 190 pages

● **JEFF JANSSEN'S PEAK PERFORMANCE PLAYBOOK**　　　**Team Building Pkg Price $49.95 - Save $5**
  50 Drills, Activities & Ideas to Inspire Your Team, Build Mental Toughness & Improve Team Chemistry
  This playbook details 50 effective, economical, and easy to use mental game and team building drills for your team. The playbook comes complete with drill objectives, setup instructions, step by step directions, follow-up discussion questions, and master handouts. $24.95, 82 pages

● **THE MENTAL MAKINGS OF CHAMPIONS workbook**
  This innovative workbook breaks down the strategies of mental training into practical and easy to use worksheets. Learn how you can quickly and easily incorporate mental training into your everyday practices and games. Makes a great complement to the WTMG video. $19.95, 50 pages
  Team Package: Save 25% when you buy 10 or more workbooks for your team. Only $14.95 per workbook + a free WTMG video ($12 ship).

● **WINNING THE MENTAL GAME video**　　　**Champion's Pkg Price $39.95 - Save $10**
  How You Can Develop the Motivation, Confidence & Focus of Champions
  This video teaches athletes and coaches how to Master The Mental Game for success in sport, school, and the game of life. $29.95, VHS/48 min. *Champion's Package: Save $10 when you order the video and workbook - only $39.95.*

● **THE SEVEN SECRETS OF SUCCESSFUL COACHES book**
  Learn how to get the absolute most out of your players using the coaching strategies of sport's most successful coaches including Pat Summitt, Mike Krzyzewski, Mike Candrea, and many others. Discover how to create confident, consistent, and coachable athletes. $29.95, 224 pages

● **THE TEAM CAPTAIN'S LEADERSHIP MANUAL**
  The Complete Guide to Developing Team Leaders Who Coaches Respect and Teammates Trust
  This proven manual includes a 10 week program to help you develop more responsible and respected team captains. Develop vocal leaders who will set the tone for your team, hold teammates accountable, constructively confront less disciplined teammates, refocus teammates when they are down or distracted, and take care of team problems so you don't have to. $29.95 (2-9 copies $24.95 each, 10 or more copies $19.95 each)

● **BUILDING A WINNING TEAM CHEMISTRY video**
  Discover a proven game plan for building your team's chemistry, confidence, and commitment. $29.95, VHS/50 min.

● **THE PERFORMANCE ZONE E-MAIL NEWSLETTER**
  Receive a wealth of peak performance tips and techniques delivered monthly via e-mail. This cutting edge newsletter keeps you up to date with the latest strategies for building mental toughness and team chemistry. $29.95 for 10 issues (1 yr), $49.95 for 20 issues (2 yr)

Visit www.jeffjanssen.com for more information.

Deluxe Package - Save $30 and get all 8 of Jeff's resources for only $195

Peak Performance Products Order Form

Item	Price	Quantity	Subtotal

Order Today!
Satisfaction Guaranteed

Name_____

Team/Sport_____

Address_____

City, State, Zip_____

Phone_____ E-mail_____

Shipping

NC residents add 7%

Shipping: $5.00 1st it $1.00 each add. item

TOTAL

Credit Card #_____ Exp._____

Signature_____

Send your check, money order, or purchase order payable in U.S. dollars to:

Janssen Peak Performance, Inc., 6841 Piershill Lane, Cary, NC 27519

For quick & easy credit card orders call toll free 1-888-721-TEAM fax (919) 303-4338 or on-line at www.jeffjanssen.com